# singing about melon

# Luke Thompson

# *Singing About Melon*

Shearsman Books

First published in the United Kingdom in 2020 by
Shearsman Books Ltd
PO Box 4239
Swindon
SN3 9FN

Shearsman Books Ltd Registered Office
30–31 St. James Place, Mangotsfield, Bristol BS16 9JB
*(this address not for correspondence)*

www.shearsman.com

ISBN 978-1-84861-735-3

Cover image, 'Ascension', copyright © Mairead Dunne, 2020.

# CONTENTS

*for sarah*

SILENZIO
SILENZIO
SILENZIO

## Three Poems

*after Lafcadio Hearn's 'Insect Musicians'*

'Let us go insect-hunting tonight,' the poet said.
'It will be dark and I have many lanterns ready.'


do not
leave the city

cicadas and crickets
in bamboo cages

eating melon rind
singing about melon

on a spring night
Kiriyama hears
still, small voices
risen from clay

a ghost-song in the jar
where our parents died

and at my funeral
the cage will open

but instead of insects
lizards and birds
singing

Sitting in the shade of lime trees
on the piazza of Santa Chiara.
Swifts scream in the olive grove.

A leaf falls

Rondini     silenziosi
Rondoni     rumoroso

# Mouth

words scatter
like birds
when I speak

the moon
rolls down
my tongue

salt on my lips
a ship's hull
pressed to the sea

each word
dressed in feathers

each word
a waking bat

a waking bat
hanging from the roof
of my mouth

the wings of a parakeet
beat in my puffed cheeks

hollow
as a lobster

my mouth a bowl, full
of seahorses

the sea
pours through
my teeth

my tongue
a river
of eels

a sea of eels
lapping the shore

words slither
up the berm
of my lips

spider crabs
hammer
at my teeth

my teeth
a row
of uncarved slates

an ulcer
in my cheek
a moon

an egg
on my tongue

my tongue a bear
my teeth flames
in the circus

elephants wearing garters
and feathered skull caps circle
the sawdust floor of my mouth

a bear in a coloured ruff
and muzzle pedals a bicycle

I lace the kangaroo's gloves
tying them with cherry stalks

my teeth a troupe
of polar bears
with scarred noses

my teeth a train of wagons
transporting lions,
tigers, bears and dogs

releasing exotic birds
on my breath

puffins nest
in the burrow
of my throat

on my tongue
an abandoned egg

my tongue
a murmuration of starlings
falling to roost

on my tongue
a forest of words

and within it a nightjar
churring

my breath
bare-beaked
rooks

each word
a hollow gall
drops from my lips

The fields were already parched
when a feather fell from the canary's cheek

# The Stopped Clocks of the Friars

*il Convento dei Cappuccini di Via Veneto*

| | | |
|---|---|---|
| 5.20 | 12.11 | 7.43 |
| 10.23 | 8.49 | – |
| 3.45 | 5.20 | 5.08 |
| 8.38 | 5.03 | 5.30 |
| 12.55 | 9.44 | 3.01 |
| 3.11 | 7.09 | 12.10 |
| 1.23 | 9.06 | 10.39 |
| 2.27 | 4.05 | 8.17 |
| 8.24 | 9.25 | |

SUPERIORE
INFERIORE
TOMBA

# The Goal of All Life is Death

*a speculative sonnet essay*

One of my favourite cryptozoology books is Kenneth Gandar-Dower's *The Spotted Lion*. I don't think it will ruin the book to tell you he does not find a spotted lion and there is probably no such thing.

Do you remember in psychology when you were told about the man who was hunting deer and had not seen any deer but was looking so hard for deer that when he saw a person instead of seeing a person he saw a deer and shot them?

Freud ended his teenage years by pulling apart European eels in search of their testicles. It was his first academic post and it is said he dismantled 400 eels in his search for their testicles.

The problem was that eels do not have testicles until they need them and by then they are on their way back to the Sargasso Sea. No one knew this when Freud started deconstructing eels.

With every action taken we are faced with either the pain of failure or the dullness of satiation. So will and desire come from suffering and they lead to suffering, Schopenhauer says.

In the Sargasso Sea male eels grow testicles. They fuck and they die. Eros and Thanatos. The lack of testicles in the eels he unstitched was a trauma Freud would relive time and again.

## Robot Squirrel

Zooming in with his telescopic eyes, Robot Squirrel watched a neighbour drinking. Its muzzle touched the water and its slender tongue wiggled in and out, tapping the puddle as it moved to and from the flesh squirrel's mouth.

Robot Squirrel admired the ripples expanding across the water's surface, caused by the flesh squirrel's tongue. He opened his own mouth and inserted a birch leaf.

Robot Squirrel approached the puddle.
He looked down into it.

In the reflection
he watched
his metal jaw open,
his head bow,
and as it did so
he watched
his new birch leaf tongue
　　　slide out
　　　　　　and spin
　　　　　　　　　across the surface of the puddle.

　　　　　　*At least*, thought Robot Squirrel,
　　　　　　*I have mastered the ripples.*

## Two Craneflies

As two crane flies struggle to free themselves, trapped as they are between the flysheet and the inner of the tent, their legs accidentally touch and each instinctively recoils.

One leg breaks off, then another, until they are no longer able to move.

How did we get here?

# Sacrament of Reconciliation

Forgive me father for I
Have sinned for me father
Me I forgive father have
I forgive me for father
Forgive father for me I
Father me for I have
Sinned for me father

## Migrations of the Silver Eel

in the moon we come up we go out and we drink we make ourselves a fool · we fight on the garage forecourt · in the bus light richard sings that loving feeling again we come up waxed exceeding mighty · we get out at holmbush we walk exceeding mighty to carlyon bay friends honk their horns as they pass they are what they are · the moon drew him out of the water · waxed · lights the (i am) river-moist road we dance in the stars and in the bay on the beach we swim out together and richard catches chlamydia mighty we swim in the midst of the sea and he sings and we lie in the (i am) sand as the moon falls we bury ourselves in the sand as the moon falls

The birds scatter
like words. Jackdaws
and gulls that followed
the plough, plucking cockchafer
larvae from soft furrows.

the lizard in the grotto
hears a leaf fall

## To a Woodlouse

*looking for a reflection in the bird bath / I find you, pale and saturated*

    You drank through your ass and mouth, heading home

    and water soaked in through your shell a way you don't remember

    and so you died, imbibing, hungry as a black hole

*I know your joy / those moments we walk weightless / across the slate*

from *The Cloud of Unknowing*

God, that is giver
of time, giveth never
two times together,

but one
after
another.

## Robot Squirrel II

In place of the birch leaf tongue, Robot Squirrel affixed a twig, which he could rotate like a whisk.

*No squirrel makes ripples like Robot Squirrel.*

| | | | | | | | |
|---|---|---|---|---|---|---|---|
| par | ak | eet | par | ak | eet | par | rot |
| rot | eet | par | rot | eet | par | rot | par |
| par | par | ak | par | par | ak | par | rot |
| rot | rak | eet | rot | ak | eet | rot | par |
| par | eet | par | par | eet | par | par | rot |
| rot | par | ak | rot | par | ak | rot | par |
| par | ak | eet | par | ak | eet | par | rot |
| rot | eet | par | rot | eet | par | rot | par |

| pa  | rr   | ot  | ts  | p   | ar  | ro  | ts  |   |
|-----|------|-----|-----|-----|-----|-----|-----|---|
| rr  | ots  | pa  | r   | r   | ots | ts  | p   |   |
| ots | pa   | r   | ro  | ts  | p   | a   | a   |   |
| p   | r    | r   | r   | o   | ar  | s   | rt  |   |
| pa  | pa   | rr  | rr  | ro  | o   | ts  | s   |   |
| r   | rts  | o   | o   | os  | pa  | s   | t   |   |
| p   | a    | ar  | ar  | t   | s   | s   | o   | o |
| pa  | ra   | ts  | pa  | ar  | ts  |     | p   |   |
|     |      |     |     |     |     |     | s   |   |

# Here am I

Before dawn the sound of a voice woke me.
I said 'Speak, for thy servant heareth'.
It was a woodpigeon.

Night rain, still in the trees
slapped through the leaves.

A line of blackbirds scratched in the laurel.
Roe deer crashed about the beechwood.

'Here am I', I whispered
because it was not yet light.

# The Egg of the Eel

A comma trapped in a full stop
An earthworm in an apple
A river inside a balloon

A breeze turns the pages of the newspaper
while I sleep in the sun. A butterfly
pauses on an apple leaf.

When I wake
the news
is over.

# Robot Squirrel III

Robot Squirrel sat in the snow. He had been waiting for days.

He was staring at a crack in an ancient oak on the edge of the woods, before the field and the farm and the gardener's cottage, because in that crack in the oak on the edge of the woods was a drey; a winter bed, thick and warm. The young squirrel that had constructed the drey rarely came out.

Robot Squirrel sat in the snow. He had been waiting for days.

On the sixth day, she moved. She stuck out her nose. Then it disappeared again. In and out. A little further. Further and further. Before long, she showed herself fully. She clung to the tree, paused, then scrambled down the trunk and around the field to the cottage. Robot Squirrel watched her hopping through the pasture, each bound taking her closer to the imagined seed and the bird feeder, each squat hiding her from something else imagined.

When he was sure she was gone, Robot Squirrel clattered over to the tree and up the trunk to the crack in the ancient oak. He pushed his head inside and lit up the drey with his LED eyelights.

*Oh, you exquisite creature*, Robot Squirrel exclaimed.

Inside the cavity dry branches from hazel trees, beech, birch and ash were pressed and woven and crushed together, making angles complex as crystal formations and steaming with warmth. The bowl of the nest was packed with thistledown, moss, sheep's wool and feathers, smoothed down where the squirrel had been curled up asleep.

*This is how we winter!*

With this new understanding, Robot Squirrel dashed down the trunk and for the rest of the day he ran about, scraping moss from the trees and the old stone wall by the river, and sticks from the woodland floor. He built his drey high up in the crook of an ash, weaving it together just like the flesh squirrel had done, in beautiful, complex, crystalline patterns, and he stuffed the crevices with the gathered moss. Late in the afternoon, Robot Squirrel's drey was ready. He crawled inside the crook of the ash and lay down. But as careful as he tried to be, the twigs creaked and snapped beneath him, the moss squashed flat, and within seconds the drey was ruined.

For the rest of the evening, Robot Squirrel sat on a branch in a neighbouring beech, looking back at his broken drey and wondering what went wrong. It was dark by the time he made his decision.

Through the night, Robot Squirrel dashed about the hedgerows, farmyard, barns and dumps, gathering up chicken wire and tarpaulin, roofing felt and a small orange tilt bucket with broken teeth. Robot Squirrel built his drey, lined it with gravel and snuggled in. He felt neither warmer nor colder.

# Cratylus and the Eel

**Eel**: What sense does it make to say language has no meaning?

**Cratylus**: [waggles finger positively]

**Eel**: Are you trying to say something?

**Cratylus**: [waggles finger negatively]

**Eel**: What is that? Is that a language?

**Cratylus**: [finger stops moving]

**Eel**: Is that meant to be me?

**Cratylus**: [unwaggles finger]

# Migrations of the Silver Eel II

The moon has been waning
more than a year, becoming
newer and newer

the river empties
and the grass parts

entangled in the wilderness
*you've changed*

I have been here, I think,
too long

# Anchorite

Entomb me.
Seal me up.

Stud my cell
with flint.

Let me dig
a grave

with my
fingertips

and practice lying
there.

Feed me.
Let me live

my death
a little more.

I went out
again tonight

sat in the layby
on the hill

to call home
to hear you say

you're sorry
that you're not in

right now

A neighbour called by
to say a burglar
broke in her place
today. 'Did he take
much?' I asked.

'Nothing,' she said. 'I thought
I ought to tell you.'

But what about the certainty that the sun will rise

  "     "                                    "    "

  "    "    "    "                              "

                          "    "    "    "

    "    "            "

    "    "    "    "

# Ivy-Leaved Toadflax

*a triptych*

flowers pour down Rabbit's beard like oil
bell bronze on limestone
washing along the walls in prayer

Rabbit says, 'Behold,
how good and how pleasant

for us to dwell together
in unity!'

Rabbit's head wilts on the stalk
presses a rotten face into a crevice
in the wall
                rises Rabbit

## Robot Squirrel IV

Robot Squirrel cannot scream to attract a mate. All he can manage is a weak hydraulic hiss. But he can bang a stick against his legs, head and back to make three attractive sounds. *Tink. Thunk. Dong.*

## My Speech is now Decay'd

'I don't know how you're doing it,'
you say, believing this is all a simulation of home.
'If this is really real, go out to the garden
where I can see you, and cut me
the flower from the top of that tree.'
I wave at you through the window,
climb the tree and cut the flower.
'I don't know how you're doing it.'

You say: 'Ali's up the artificial tree eating an unctuous pear.'
You say: 'There are ducks bigger than me out there.'
You say: 'It would be a good place to fix up the radio. The original one from years
back. In the squirrels' house where it used to be. It has transmitter and receiver now.'
You say: 'There are more shadows in the room today.'

Fragments of exotic birds
crowd the hospital feeder,
parrots and parakeets.

# In the Mint Bed

To which god

or priest of god

does one confess

that one pissed

in the mint bed?

# Ventriloquist

"A ventriloquist
ventriloquises
but more than this is
a ventriloquist"
*online dictionary*

Bottle of beer
Bottle of beer
Bottle of beer
Bottle of beer

Bottle of beer
Bottle of beer
Bottle of beer
Bottle of beer

Gottle a geer
Gottle a geer
Gottle a geer

Am I?

am I here
to underscore
your vigour?

your eyebrows rigid
teeth clenched
glance distant

Am I?

without me
you would look
so stupid right now

I am

whose voice?

Without me you would be just
some weirdo pulling faces
on a stage

"Aw, are you sad?"
you joke. The crowd
plays along, groaning.
"Have I hurt your feelings?"

How do you sleep
in the knowledge
of what you made me say
and do?

## Robot Squirrel V

Trying to improve himself –
to soothe his jangle and master his yawp –
Robot Squirrel took apart
his brother squirrels
and sister squirrels
in the woods.

He fixed their teeth along his back and face
and tied three real tails to his rump.

But Robot Squirrel looked less
like a squirrel
and felt more alone
than ever.

would you come back
fragments of exotic words
gathered around the feeder

parrots and parakeets
on the ward

would you come back
before I could carry you

before they carried you
out
        on a gurney

wheels crunching through the gravel

leaving fur
row marks

in the dr
i
ve


Wo
uld

it

see
m

gr
ace
le
ss

to fetch
the rake?

# Forget the Whole Created World

| | | | | | |
|---|---|---|---|---|---|
| Forgetting | Forgetting | Forgetting | Forgetting | Forgetting | Forgetting |
| Forgetting | Forgetting | Forgetting | Forgetting | Forgetting | Forgetting |
| Forgetting | Forgetting | Forgetting | Forgetting | Forgetting | Forgetting |
| Forgetting | Forgetting | Forgetting | Forgetting | Forgetting | Forgetting |
| Forgetting | Forgetting | Forgetting | Forgetting | Forgetting | Forgetting |
| Forgetting | Forgetting | Forgetting | Forgetting | Forgetting | Forgetting |
| Forgetting | Forgetting | Forgetting | Forgetting | Forgetting | Forgetting |
| Forgetting | Forgetting | Forgetting | Forgetting | Forgetting | Forgetting |
| Forgetting | Forgetting | Forgetting | Forgetting | Forgetting | Forgetting |
| Forgetting | Forgetting | Forgetting | Forgetting | Forgetting | Forgetting |
| Forgetting | Forgetting | Forgetting | Forgetting | Forgetting | Forgetting |
| Forgetting | Forgetting | Forgetting | Forgetting | Forgetting | Forgetting |
| Forgetting | Forgetting | Forgetting | Forgetting | Forgetting | Forgetting |
| Forgetting | Forgetting | Forgetting | Forgetting | Forgetting | Forgetting |
| Forgetting | Forgetting | Forgetting | Forgetting | Forgetting | Forgetting |
| Forgetting | Forgetting | Forgetting | Forgetting | Forgetting | Forgetting |
| Forgetting | Forgetting | Forgetting | Forgetting | Forgetting | Forgetting |
| Forgetting | Forgetting | Forgetting | Forgetting | Forgetting | Forgetting |
| Forgetting | Forgetting | Forgetting | Forgetting | Forgetting | Forgetting |
| Forgetting | Forgetting | Forgetting | Forgetting | Forgetting | Forgetting |
| Forgetting | Forgetting | Forgetting | Forgetting | Forgetting | Forgetting |
| Forgetting | Forgetting | Forgetting | Forgetting | Forgetting | Forgetting |

You say you are green
I say I am verdigris
You say you are blue
I say I am mallard neck

You say you are red
I say I am arterial blood red
I say I am head of the cock goldfinch red

You say you are white
I say I am the inside quill feathers of the kittiwake
I say I am smoke grey
I say I am flesh fly
I say I am leek green
I say I am canary bird
I say I am gallstones
I say I am polar bear
I say I am the eggs of the flesh fly
I say I am the dead leaves of green panic grass

# Into

a flower into a fruit
a forest into a city
a rabbit into a soup

a poem from a squid
a necklace from a bed of oysters
a grave from a hole

a noose from a tow rope
a mouse from sugar
an enemy from a friend

something into nothing
nothing into something

# Little Star

*after 'small stars', in the Book of Songs*

I am the little star
writhing in the
night.

I am the little star
quivering in the
dark.

I am the little
star hovering in
the sky.

I am the little star.
By morning I must be gone.

# Low Tide at Charlestown

A girl sits
on the rocks
limpet between her legs
pressing at it with both thumbs

No,
her father says,
that's not how you do it.
Put your shoes back on.

We'll leave
that one
for now.

They walk along the rocks. Here,
says the father. Watch.

He kicks the limpet
at the base of its shell
and it flies
pitching off
down the pebble beach.

The girl has a go
and crushes
the first
one.

Careful! Not like that,
says the father. Like this.

And the pair move off
out of earshot.

I watched the priest drop his McDonald's milkshake on the subway steps and I watched it dry in the sun, a candyfloss-coloured fresco secco

# The Last Supper

According to the *Daily Mail* Jesus ate eels.
No, I don't mean the *Daily Mail*. I mean

Leonardo da Vinci. Leonardo da Vinci
ate eels. He possessed at least one cook book

and that contained a recipe for eels.
He was a vegetarian so he didn't exactly

eat eels, but if he could have eaten eels
they would have been done with orange.

Or rather, when Leonardo da Vinci
painted Jesus eating eels they were cooked

with orange. Jesus ate eels with orange –
or lemon – at the Last Supper, according

to Leonardo da Vinci. Unless it was
someone else who ordered the eel that day.

# Migrations of the Silver Eel III

had an uneasy dream i dreamed you were leaving me and you walked away and you wouldnt turn back and when i woke and i reached out for you you were gone and i remember you are dead and the rest of the night i will not sleep the rest of the night and beg god i were walking with you the rest of the night and theres no morning coming and i hear three flies moving upon the face of the water and i grab the first fly with my hand and place it on the bedside table and there is no light and i think i am drifting but im not im swimming and i grab the second fly with my hand and place it on the bedside table and i thought someone said your name but it was an echo and i grab the third fly with my hand and place it on the bedside table and i scoop up all three flies and stick them up my nose one by one and i inhale so deeply and the flies wake in the night of my lungs and clatter about turning and turning the rest of the night and i try to remember your voice but i dont remember any words you used if you used any words and i think of your tongue and i listen to the sound of the flies in my lungs in the night of your rest in your rest in your tongue that nights down my throat and curls like a river and rests in my lung and im leaving the forest leaving the river leaving the fields leaving the turtle that scuds through the rest of the night or i am not or i am i am not i am without your words or i am one breath in the water or one word in the water in the tongue of the night in the tongue of the rest in the tongue of

Time hatches
from the back
of the Surinam toad

one moment
after another

# Anchorite II

*deprive*

deer
deep
pride

de

re

rip
rive
peer
dive

de
pride
re
pride

re
rive
de
rive

de
deep
re
deep

re
rip
de
rip

d
rip
dr
ip
dri
p

# Dear Fish Hair

*homophonic translation of*
*Johann Wolfgang von Goethe's 'Der Fischer'*

Dishwasher rushed, dishwasher swole
And fish sauce therein
So necked them and jelly roll.
Cool Biscuits hurt his hand
And wire systems vie for laughs.
Tight sickly flute emperor
Has a Bewick swan weather house
Evicted with fervour

She sang to him 'Seaspray Zoo Hymn';
What loss to my beauty!
Made mention with a Dalmatian lost
Enough in the despot.
As weird as you, my fishline is,
So won't lick off the ground.
Dusted her under. Why dubious?
A word is testament.

Lastly, deliver sunny night;
Demand cygnet in me.
Carved walnut man urges it.
Night toppled sooner here.
Look, ditch-dirty fur inglenook,
Daft folk work the table.
Look, deep down, I can almost see
Knitted heron. Who can tell?

Dishwasher rushed, dishwasher swole.
Nasty damn knackered foot.
Sinners will sin, oh sausage vole,
Obey the lips then grab Sauce.
Preach zoo hymns, singsong zoo hymns.
There was one, I'm guessing,
Who, not seeing her, thanked heaven
Underneath my cousin.

Jesus sat on the moon
tossing angels at earth
like playing cards in a top hat

There's smoke over the farm. The barn roof glows
every night the same in the evening sun.

Butterflies cover the peppermint flowers. Unripe
apples have fallen all over the clover.

Wasps crowd the split pipe, drinking from the gash,
one after another, water bleeding down in the drought.

There are bees and thin-limbed spiders
and ants in three colours, yellow, red and black.

Sarah will be home from work soon.
I'll hear her stamping through the woods,

the gate and the latch, the gravel beneath her feet.
I hardly leave the garden anymore.

# The Final Migration of the Silver Eel

Deep in the forest a call, a long-drawn howl:
*I thirst*

and I always said
I'd never do it

led by the night
squeezing into Spanx
and consuming my own organs

I empty myself,
chew on the days we plucked pulses
from the apple trees

all cares left behind
forgotten in the lilies

I clear my throat and my tongue falls out

*I thirst*

chew my face smooth
suck my skull thin as shell

*I thirst*

not the death in the pickle jar or nailed to a door
salted and flayed and hung on the smoker's line

and I always said I'd never do it
led by the night

in the smell of the choir
the song of the parched sea

you were just skin and eggs
and that was all I wanted

# Acknowledgements

'Three Poems' is a response to Lafcadio Hearn's essay 'Insect Musicians'. These poems were published on *in every year* and in *PN Review*. 'The Stopped Clocks of the Friars' is composed of times transcribed from the watches of friars who died in *il Convento dei Cappuccini di Via Veneto*. The watches are on display in the monastery's museum, which also includes the more famous series of chapels decorated with thousands of bones and skeletons. This piece was exhibited at Tremenheere Sculpture Gardens in the Kate Walters show in 2019, along with the 'Mouth' sequence and the 'Final Migration of the Silver Eel'. 'Migrations of the Silver Eel II' first appeared in *Reliquiae*, November 2019. Versions of the 'Robot Squirrel' poems first appeared in the zimZalla pamphlet *Robot Squirrel*, illustrated by John Kilburn. The eel poems also emerged from working with John on the Suitcase Full of Eels collaboration, supported by the Sustainable Earth Institute and Sustainable Eel Group. 'Two Craneflies' was first published by *PN Review*, alongside 'My Speech is now Decay'd'. 'Ivy-Leaved Toadflax' was written for *The Wandering Heath* anthology, edited by Honeysuckle Troubridge, Gabby Willcox, Amber Patterson and Josie Heaton. 'Dear Fish Hair' was first published in the *New Networks for Nature 2018* anthology. There are references throughout to a range of texts, including the mystical *Cloud of Unknowing*, Julian of Norwich's *Revelations of Divine Love*, John of the Cross's *Dark Night of the Soul* and *Werner's Nomenclature of Colour*.

The title of 'My Speech is now Decay'd' is a line from Robert Herrick's 'Litany to the Holy Spirit'. In 'Little Star', the stars in the original poem were the master's handmaids who, like stars, would need to disappear by dawn.

Thanks are owed to the editors, curators and artists involved in these projects, as well as to the friends who have read and encouraged the writing. Thank you.

Lightning Source UK Ltd.
Milton Keynes UK
UKHW030401240920
370397UK00006B/121

9 781848 617353